Follies and Crowns

a poetry collection by

Kayley Nicole

Follies and Crowns

Copyright © 2025 by Kayley Nicole

All rights reserved. No part of this book may be reproduced in any form without permission from the author or publisher, except as permitted by U.S. copyright law.

To request permission, contact
kayleynicolepoetry@gmail.com

Cover art and section break art: Endrju

*To those who stayed.
I needed you.
I love you.*

Author's Note

This collection of poetry centers on my journey through a situational major depressive episode, which overtook my life for well over a year. Some poems involve themes of pregnancy loss, abuse, suicide, and depression. Please be mindful of these potential triggers and proceed with caution.

I created this collection primarily for myself—to symbolically close a chapter of my life while stepping into a new one. If you've found this collection, I'm offering a shared human experience of loss, nostalgia, heartbreak, the effects of repressed trauma, healing, self-love, and creating art.

Some poems are quite straightforward. Others I attempted to string together more delicately. Writing helped me work through and process my emotions during a tumultuous time. It gave me an outlet when I felt like there was nowhere else to turn.

I can't promise quality. I wrote from all kinds of emotions and through brain fog, depending on what kind of day, week, or month I was having. I didn't want to change too much. Life doesn't work that way. I can't go back and change an experience. I didn't want to pretend I was writing from the darkest moments of my life only to have rewritten them from the other side.

    I am on the other side now. It was a long road, and to anyone still on it—please stay on it. There are brighter days ahead. I am so grateful to the version of me who grasped and held onto life while simultaneously wanting to let go, so I could bask in the light of today, with a lovely promise of tomorrow.

Table of Contents

Glimpses of Before 1

Descending 22

Shimmers of Light 62

Creation 88

Epilogue 101

Acknowledgements 103

About the Author 104

Follies and Crowns

Glimpses of Before

Merlot in the Bathtub

We drink to the stars!
You'll find me unarmed—here.
The party stopped,
and onward I danced
beneath the glow of Selene.

In the grove, I solitarily roam,
my feet halting to pick a daisy.
As I admired her beauty,
I fell through the hole
I had left behind in the earth.

As I descended,
I yearned
to be seen—
completely,
effortlessly.

What is a mind unburdened,
slipping between all space and time?

Cusp of Magic

Traveling back in time,
it was proper to be fair and pale—
to display the delicacy of a female.
But I'd cut off all my hair
so the sun could lay me bare,
among raspberries dangling from the vine,
eating each voluptuous berry, one at a time—
sweet and tangy of summertime's best.

The sun soaks in and warms my breasts.
The ground beneath a billowy tree
becomes my bed,
a crown of lilies resting upon my head.
Atop brown hair lightening to gold—
I'm a sight to behold.

Cherry Lips

Born and raised
under the green mountains
on a stormy summer's day.

Feet sliding on slick rocks in creek beds.
Wading up to the knees.
Sun shining through trees.

Picking berries.
Holding kittens.
Pausing time.

Blonde hair blowing in the wind.
Spare change turned into cotton candy ice cream.
Bike wheels spinning.

Evolving into cherry lipstick.
Pearl necklaces.
Turning heads.

Rocks thrown at an attic bedroom window.
Beckoning from below.
Streetlights.

A shadowed grin.

A feeling of sin.

The Song of Two Sisters

On a crisp autumn morning,
two sisters sang a song.
Their harmonies were carried
on a gust of swirling wind filled with
orange,
crimson red,
and yellow leaves.

The sisters loved to sing—both together and apart.
For as long as they could remember,
they loved to emote in song.
They spent their days
crafting harmonies and melodies,
like their own little soliloquies.

They were the daughters of autumn,
fluttering about,
climbing the mountain hills
shrouded in the colors of change:
the orange,
the crimson red,
and the yellows.
They spent their days endlessly in song,
carried on the wind,
echoing through the meadows.

As the air turned to bitter cold,
Winter came bustling through.
The eldest sister was separated
from the youngest sister—

forever.
Never to be reunited again.
The eldest sister entered a long winter's sleep.
The youngest sister's song froze in her throat,
for one cannot sing with no joy in their heart.
Years passed without song.

Autumn's wind carried nothing but leaves.
Winter's howl brought only frigid air,
stinging and drawing tears from the eyes.
Summer's sun offered nothing but stifling heat.
Spring appeared—then quickly passed.

Thus, the years flew by until, at last, one spring,
her song began to thaw
as the tulips began to sprout.
Slowly,
melting away
like honey dripping from the comb.

When the young woman breathed in
and began to sing,
she didn't recognize the sound of her voice.
It was coarse—
deeper than before.

Her song was forever changed by the winter,
aged by the weight of grief
from the loss of her autumn sister.
No wind carried her song.
No one harmonized beside her.

But for a brief moment,
as the air filled her lungs,
she recalled her eldest sister's song.
She could hear it from memory once more.

And that was enough.

Front Street

I'm going to drive past the house
we were last a family in.
A mourning dove stands in the road,
wheels spinning past the tree
we climbed to rescue another kitten.

I follow the creek
our little feet splashed in.
I pass the blackberry bushes
we used to pluck
until our fingertips turned purple.

Jostling with the potholes,
accelerating up the hill,
I slow down.
I look at the solitary brick mass
centered on barren land.

They cut all the trees down—
trees that housed campfires and mirth,
branches shading the swimming pool
on blistering sunny afternoons.
Now, only bulbous circular stumps remain.

I look up.
On summer nights,
I'd slip out the basement door,
walk through dew-sodden grass.
I'd lean back and look up at the sky.

I'd count all the constellations I could find —
start with the North Star,
then the Big Dipper,
then the Little Dipper,
until starry eyes landed on my favorite, Cassiopeia.

In this tiny little town,
I could see it all
while lost under the moonlight.
Breaking my solitude and woes,
I'd tiptoe back in.

I'd drift off to sleep
with snores heard
through shared walls —
a white noise
I had never lived without.

Leaving the desolate brick,
I descend the hill.
I brake at the stop sign
and merge where the impact occurred —
a block, and you'd be home.

With my heart sinking,
I mutter, "They cut all the trees down."

Was It All Gray?

I remember colors,
rainbows
with sparkles.

I remember skinned knees
and suntan lines,
fighting with the wind to fly a kite.

I remember playing with dolls,
and playing library,
with books leaned against walls.

I remember giggles
and playing pretend,
fighting over our favorite Ken.

With each other we were safe.
With each other,
my happiness didn't fade.

The Incurable Ache

Pink lines.
Bedside table
littered with Tums.
Needles, pills, giant water jugs.
Chicken noodle soup
for weeks on end.
Your heartbeat—
instinctively knowing:
you're my son.

Winnie the Pooh swaddle,
bedtime stories.
Waiting
in an empty room
you never got to discover.

Fruitless

My womb will never bear any fruit—
so I planted strawberry vines
and raspberry bushes.
Toiling in the soil,
I built garden walls.
Nimble fingers pulling weeds
and rescuing tired bumblebees;
I cover myself in dirt,
and I breathe life into the earth.

I pull tomatoes from the vine.
I cut cucumbers
one
at
a
time.

I give pollen to the bees,
while birds peck at sunflower seeds.
Watching butterflies in the wildflower patch,
I pick a raspberry—ripe at last—
and I savor all this color I've birthed
from what was once an empty square of dirt.

Venus

You carved into me like marble,
chisel in hand,
shaping curves into unfulfilled dreams,
and long since wasted away
fantasies.

The Good Days

Can I stay in this moment,
forever, with you?
The shadows and black clouds above us part
to let the gleam and warmth of sunlight
grace our hearts.
Throw open the blinds!
Let the world watch our love.

These are the days
I've been dreaming of.
Let's take off our boxing gloves.
My heart is yours.
Your hand leaves
an imprint on my soul.
Does mine do the same to you?

This rapture, this entanglement—
I can't picture feeling this way
for only a fleeting day.
The highs are high and soaring above.
Do we have to fall,
or can we learn to spread our wings
and rise above it all?
Above it all.

On the good days,
I still remember the falls.
I brace myself for the next brawl.
Brushing your hair off your shoulder,
resting my cheek in the crook of your neck—
I know what I'm holding on for.
How long will you let me stay here?

Moon Girl

It's Selene and me,
walking through this life—
with pain shared in whispers,
thrown in bottles
out to sea.
And with the tides,
the moon brings my love
back to me.

How Long Is Forever?
Tall brown trunks,
green in between.
Smoke rises
from the chimney.

Mountain ranges,
sunlight over Keuka Lake.
Crickets chirping.
White paws resting on knees.

Wooden walls,
torn hearts
healing beneath
cloudy blue skies.

Night falls.
I stoke the fire.
We watch the stars.
I fall asleep in your arms.

We nap.
We laugh.
We kiss—
like old times.

Under the canopy of green,
I forget my heartache.
The strings of my heart
reach out for yours.

Still, I hesitate.

Enraptured

I always say being with her
is like seeing loud and vibrant colors—
but what if I told you
I saw those colors
with her head between my thighs,
eyes closed,
toes curled,
and my back arched toward the sky?

Essence

You don't like my garden
or my houseplants.
You don't like my poetry
or book collections.

You don't like when I rhyme,
or when I think about spending a dime—
even if it's mine.
You don't like my body.

You don't like my 'girlie' trinkets,
my baggy shirts,
or when I listen to music
while washing your dishes.

When I talk to you,
it's like I'm wasting your time.
Why do you cage me,
if you don't like me?

False Hope
A sordid past.
A broken glass.
Despite the pain inflicted,
love was bountiful.

The girl loved the girl loved the girl.

Out of the darkness,
a ray of light shimmered through,
bringing forth
a new day.

An iris grew
out of the blue.

Follies and Crowns

Descending

Clouded

Is there hope for me and you?
Is the iris still blooming out of the blue?
Are the petals shriveled and brown?
Is it wilted—did it drown?

Can we plant bulbs
to lift the fog,
blooming in spring,
when we'll both wear our rings?

If I still bleed,
will you scatter forget-me-not seeds
around our home—
let them grow over my bones?

When winter comes
and the raven's caw
pierces through the wind's hum,
give me faith
in what's still to come.

The Snap

Will you pull me under
if I take my walls down?
Is your remorse sincere?
Are the apologies genuine?
Is your love real?

Do you know my love can't be bought?
Flowers, jewels, and trips
don't earn my forgiveness.

Do you know my love can't be seduced?
Kisses and sweet nothings
don't earn my forgiveness.

Do I have the strength left in me
to give you one last chance?
When I consider picking up the song and dance,
I see every earth-shattering moment—
memories refusing to be replaced.

In the end, I wasn't a person.
I was an accessory.
I was collateral.
What used to be my fault
wasn't mine.

When you awoke to the disaster,
as I was leaving,
you saw it all too.

Like ships passing in the night—
here we are.
Two different sides of a coin.
Where do I go
if it's not with you?

I know the smart thing to do
is to take an ocean's length of space from you.
But it's easier to keep living our shared lives.
The good moments are more bountiful
when you're making up for your lies.

My head is clouded.
The version of who you are now
lives in my mind
with the you I once shared a bed—
for countless dark years.

Must I reconcile the two versions of you
before I can move on with my life?
I like the new you.
Reminiscent of our early days—
hugs, kisses, and cuddles.
I want to feel safe in your arms.
I want to sweep up the eggshells,
heels bleeding from crunching beneath my feet.

But the trauma buried deep within
keeps me recoiling—
on a loop,
with no end.

Aftermath

I killed all my houseplants.
The leaves turned brown,
crumbling to dust in my hands.

The garden wasn't fertilized.
The weeds ran rampant.
The tomatoes never ripened.

Dust collected on the bookshelf.
The pen went dry.
I got lost in my mind.

Captured in a jar—
sealed tight,
with no holes for air.

Buried.
Ignored.
Forgotten.

Until the glass cracked,
succumbing to the pressure—
slowly, little by little,
engulfing me
in a haze of gray.

Chronic Recurring Thoughts of Death
I'm a little girl
who didn't heal in time,
and I retraced the steps—
laid myself down to bed,
with a braid in my hair
and fear in my heart.

I never relit my spark,
on a pillow filled with a broken dream—
of a life without
a hallway of echoing screams.

I gave haste to the chase,
with tears streaming down rosy cheeks,
hiding behind closet doors.
I was found.

The screams always sound the same—
accompanied with a grip on my face,
a thumb squeezing my cheek,
a twist of the arm,
a glass thrown,
a door without a lock,
a car without an exit,
a slap across the face,
a back to a corner,
a tug of hair,
an apology that never comes—

hanging in the air.

It's a hole in the wall,
fingerprint bruises on forearms,
bloody lips,
dragged upstairs,
a body pinning me to a bed.

Breathe,
breathe,
breathe,
breathe—

and the silent sobs,
released into the pillow,
with a plea for it all
to fade to black.

And onward it goes,
for years,
and years,
and decades.

And the figure
in the hall transforms
from one to another,
and it always enshrouds me.

And I could run
to the ends of the Earth,
transform my soul again and again,
but they will always find me.

As the panic fades,
and breathing slows,
I'm grateful the only hands
wanting to kill me
are my own.

Wings

Would you be up for one last chase?
When the whispers prove true,
will you dress me in the lightest shade of blue—
to carry me to the dreamland
and lay me to sleep?

Can you cover my scars with flowers,
and linger on my lips?
Place a yellow rose upon them.
Surround me with the scent
of the green earth.

Give me a view through billowy trees,
with slivers of sky slipping through.
Let me bear witness to birds in flight—
the ones who found their freedom
long before I.

For I never learned how to fly.
A lust for life kept me grounded,
allowing me to forget all my ghosts.
Until they pounced
all at once—

I ran.
Feet colliding with the earth,
for as long as they could withstand.
I fell.
And here I lie.

Betrayal

Horizon calls,
with the wings of a blue jay
soaring overhead.
But the depths below
harbor words sealed,
for none to hear.

The truth beckons,
as siren talons grip me
and hurl me
to the bottom of the sea—
where my words
duly drown me.

The Cage

While the room is on fire,
I watch the walls burn down.
The bricks I delicately laid crumble,
as mortar turns to chalk.

When my secrets spill out
from the ceiling—
dry ink hitting wooden planks—
I run.

While the room is on fire,
I look for an open window.
I pull myself through.
I don't look back for any survivors.

It's just me,
searching
for the nearest
body of water.

The wrath
following behind me
tears me to shreds.
Rips me apart.

I can't breathe.
I stumble
on the stones.
It found me—
and engulfed me whole.

Mourn
I turned off all the lights.
Maybe I can lie here tonight—
until I bleed into morning.

Revived Flames

Ignited once more,
the story doesn't change.
You want my physical touch;
I want your heart.

Two sides fated never to meet—
the dark side
and the light side
of the moon.

Alas, I bury the story.
Let time keep stretching on.
If all of me isn't wanted,
a single piece of me can't be had.

You would use me in the darkness
and then toss me
back out to sea—
to drown.

It will never be me.
I burn it.
I squash it.
I bury it.

This is my fate.
I did it to myself.
I am the only one to blame—
a victim of my own desires.

Foolish,
to carry an ounce of hope
when it was never me,
but always another.

Pyre

And so, I crumple the piece of paper.
I burn the page.
I can't let myself
go insane,
or feed even a flicker
of any lingering delusion.
There shouldn't be
any confusion.

Tomes

Whistling winds hum through the night,
a window cracked, welcoming crisp air,
yet my throat stays dry,
empty of song.

Breathe new life into me,
I rasp.
I've been dead for far too long,
yet I walk among the living.

These old tomes
suffocate in dust,
awaiting new stories
to haunt their spines.

By candlelight, these bones
hover over the page—
yet I have nothing
to scribe.

Diminished

Will I always be just a memory,
trapped in a golden afternoon?
My mind runs in circles around you,
and these bonds don't break—
they bend.

Memories are Daggers

Once, I slept buried under starlight,
with eyes alight, burning into mine—
pinning my soul to a moment,
stuck in time,
where synchronized
shallow breaths
shimmered and entwined
into the ether.

It was there we danced.
It was there I worshiped—
lilies spread upon the altar,
sacrificial blood of my youth.
I bled out for you.

In the darkness, I drift—
floating in the starlight,
weightless, Godless, and alone.

The Unintentional Torch

I dreamed of you,
I fear—my dear—
dressed in royal blue.

It's been years
since my eyes gazed upon your face.
I tried to imagine
the wrinkles time may have traced.

You were in my world
and seemed out of place.

I tried to find you alone,
to tell you:
it always felt so easy with you.

But every time
I peered over my shoulder,
she was there.

Yet you took me by the hand,
and we left together—
I, in my soft pink gown,
and you, in royal blue.

Because with you,
feeling was effortless—
as natural and as easy
as the air I breathe.

Every thought,
every dream,
feels traitorous
to me.

I let you go,
over and over.
My head betrays me—
and all others
I swore my heart to.

A Plea

If I'm Persephone,
tending the blooms
at the rise of spring,
and you are Hades—
with starry eyes
locked on sweetness,
alone in a world of blue—

then strike the ground open.
Swallow me whole.
Grip my soul.
Encompass me
in your essence.

I'll cherish you.
I'll fill your land
with green vines,
brightening your winter.
I'll hang your empty halls
with tapestries of floral hues.
I'll writhe in the heat of your fire.
I'll rule beside you—
fingers interlocked,
hand in hand—
until the fateful
death of the Gods.

Eternity.

An Army of One
My self-control is laughable.
The anxiety—palpable.
Better to spend every moment alone
than answer the phone.

Escape

Waves crashing over shore—
breathe in,
breathe out.

This is where the mind wanders.
Chin resting on knee,
sun warming brow.

An oasis for escape
when wrists are bound,
the screams too loud.

A quiet place
no one else can go,
no one else knows.

Sour

I don't believe in destiny.
I believe in the sun
warming the dirt.
I don't believe in fate.
I believe we all
evolved from apes.

What a freeing feeling—
knowing I wasn't born
with ties to any of you.
It was never a string
guiding you to me.
Just an animalistic urge
for you all to sink
your teeth into me.

I taste acidic—
an over-ripened lemon
rotting on the branch.
I haunt your tongue.
I seep into your brain,
where the deadened
look in my eyes
drifts into your dreams
and slowly drives you insane.

Vengeance

I am a flower,
wilting
under the weight of rain,
with petals drooping to the earth.

I want to let go of this pain—
wrap it in a box,
tie it with a bow,
and mail it to your home.

I want you to stumble upon it
on your porch,
open my gift,
and wear it as I did.

Candles

I yearned for you
to meet me—
safe and secure.

To be brought home,
to delight in your presence,
to fill the gaps of passing time.

To hear your voice,
to tell you every little thing
you missed.

But I awoke,
and I knew you weren't with me,
nor I with you.

I must be my own light
in the darkest corners
of my mind.

So I bend on wounded knees
and light
my candle of indigo.

And I walk.
Home.
Without you.

<u>Lighter</u>
It all went cold.
It all went dark.
Maybe I lost the spark.

Eve

Nights grow dark,
with a bite to the wind,
no drop of warmth
to be found within.

The scent of snow
haunts the eve of April.
My heart
tries to be faithful.

Forgotten is the scent
of summer's sweet dew
and the kiss of the sun
at high noon.

Memory fades
with the buzz of a bee,
and the sight of a leaf
on the branch of a tree.

Winter's howl buried
under skin—
lest spring
ever be let in.

Devotee

When I'm lost
in the dark crevices of my mind,
she stays.

When I lose track
of all time,
she stays.

When the door is open
and warm wind rustles the leaves
beneath a sunny sky,
she stays.

When my eyes are swollen,
and my cheeks are red,
her beckoning arms clasp around me—
and I stay.

Elsewhere

Nose in a book—
carry me away.
It's time for swordplay.

Take me to shores anew—
anything
to help me forget (you).

Rituals

If I could quell this endless well of empathy,
I could cut the thread more easily.
Until then,
We remain attached—
two souls bound to entwine,
eventually.

Blue Dawn

I'd like to come back as a fairy,
or a turtle basking in the sun,
or a sunflower stretching toward the sky,
nurturing all of nature's young.

Let me know no grief.
Let me never feel fingertips squeezing skin.
Let me float safely in anonymity—
existing only from within.

Bare

Standing naked in the dawn,
the embers grow cold.
I am more
than you deserve
to hold.

Starlight

I think I laid us to rest.
Finally.
There was nothing there for me —
really.
Only your desires were to be met.
Your feigned interest
revealed your true intent.

I dug us a shallow grave
at the top of a hillside,
where we can share the silence
and gaze dreamily into the starlight —
as we fade into darkness
before ever giving us the chance
to shine.

I'll mourn the lost potential
of what life could have been
if we had shared our happiness
with each other.

Just long enough to let the feelings flow.
Then I'll retire to our shallow graves,
where I will weather the rain.

Alone.

Entrenched
Reliving past trauma,
speaking to a stranger
on a worn couch,
surrounded by gray walls.
Squeezing a stress ball
until my fingers ache.

How long must I revisit the past
before I'm healed?
How long can I keep my head
in the clouds
between visits?

How honest can I be
before I'm sent to the hospital?
How do you heal
when you're always running from the truth?

There's too much to confront—
too much to face.
I take my shovel
and dig up what's been buried,

but when I'm done,
I'm in too deep of a hole
to resurface.

The Mercenary

I have soldiered on.
An army of one,
claimed every foot
of enemy territory.

I waited at the battlements,
and walked away alone.
When I made camp,
I set fire to every letter.

I am my own Knight of Swords.

The sun had set;
my mind grew weary.
So, I soldiered on.

Even if you came,
I wouldn't have stayed
to watch you luxuriate
in my hard-earned spoils.

I am my own Knight of Swords.

Up Here

Goodnight, my dear.
I laid you to rest.
As pullies creak,
and you descend into the earth,
I hope you realized how much I was worth.

More.

Bleed Into Blue

I'll say I'm dead,
though I manage to stay alive.
I've made it to another day—
somehow, I survived.
Maybe I'll make it out.

I know I won't be the only one
who completed the maze,
falling down and stumbling all the way—
with a broken body pulling itself through,
torn muscles, numb fingers,
and thighs constantly bruised.

Clawing my way across the finish line,
with freedom on the horizon,
I'd make it to the final day.
I'd look up to the rising sun and ask,
"What if it wasn't worth it, anyway?"

But before me, these hedges still beckon—
growing taller and darker,
with a bite to the wind.
Running, as the roses bleed into blue.

I'm tired, and everything hurts.
Each time I think I've reached the last turn,
the letdown is worse.
So I stop for a rest,
to fall back into sleep,
where my dreams are safe,

and I can't feel my feet.

Pleading with Hypnos to stop for me next,
the stars play my memories before me.
"Ah, look, but look, look right there!"
And I realize I'm all alone—
for fear, the same conclusions
will always lay me bare.

Has it been a day, a moment, or a year?

Solitary, I fought on.
Bare feet through stinging frost,
awaiting the next pounce of a lion—
springing from corners and bends,
awaiting my end.

Until I turned on the hedges,
to slash my way through—
with no promise of the light of day
peeking through.

Until, in exasperation,
I threw down my sword, now lost in snow.
Oh, in their revelry,
how the onlookers jeered!

"Oh, the drama! The insanity."
As I lay down and wept:
"Let me out!" I screamed,
until my voice cracked,
and my strength faded.
With a snap,
the map went up in flames.

The stars refocus and realign,
as water from Lethe drips from branch
to bloodshot eyes.
Lying trepid, as snowy paws gather round—
the sphinx leans down,
asking her simple riddle in jest:

"Who put you in here?"
Shivering blue lips mumble,
"I don't remember,"
as air leaves frozen lungs.

"Wrong," she hissed.

In a blink, the stars were gone.
Around the corner, the end was near—
but sleep and the sphinx
claimed our heroine,
our long-lost deer.

Follies and Crowns

Shimmers of Light

Awake

I thawed,
woken from a never-ending nightmare—
but it was real.

Nowhere to run,
no escape.
All the bridges burned.
Deserted on a barren island,
encircled by roaring waters,
tossed by storms.

No shelter from the rain.
Wet and soggy,
I mourn.

I mourn the years
I forsook my wants—
my needs.

I mourn the years
spent stressed and lonely,
while feeling unwanted.

I lie on the sand,
watching raindrops
rushing toward me.

I drown on land.

Sun

And like the flowers,
I, too, am back—
from the proverbial dead.

Morning

It's the faith of the fallen,
the mourner at the grave,
the caw of the raven,
the pattern of the rain.

It's the droplets on the windowsill,
the yellow petals of the daffodil—
recompense to the broken.
Spring has awoken.

Chapters
Turn the pages
in the garden.
My winter heart
unhardens.

April

Golden light caresses my shoulders
and warms me to the core.
My eyes are rested once more.

Green stems reach for the sky
from the depths of the soil,
new growth abounding all around—

new beginnings to be found.

The Journey

Standing on the ledge,
my eyes fall to the hole
below me.

From this vantage point,
I see how deeply my soul
burrowed into the cold, desolate earth.

The bottom, barely visible,
is nothing more than a void.
Not a single drop of sunlight
has ever touched its floor.

Holes from hands and feet
line the walls—
a vertical climb,
its imprint left behind.

Slide marks from falls
adorn the sides.
My nails bear dirt beneath
their once-shiny surface.
My knees are caked
with grime and mud.

Breathless,
relieved,
I look up—

and breathe.

Whole

Memories are tainted
by the abyss
I landed in.

Looking out, I see
every piece of myself
I dropped along the journey.

I turn to leave,
picking up each discarded scrap
as I turn my back.

I put it all back together—
puzzle pieces snapping into place
with tender love and care.

A promise:
to never forsake their beauty
again.

No one is worth such a grave sacrifice.
What's right will fit with me—
organically.

There will be no
reshaping
of myself.

Hollow Hauntings

In my moments of darkness,
I wanted to be saved.
I fabricated a dream—
one not so easily erased.
But now,
I must create a reality
so vibrant,
so joyful,
so safe,
I'll no longer need
a pretend place to hide.

Even when I feel trapped,
my burdens are mine to bear.
I must grow.
I must be the light
in the corners of my mind
where I run.
I must greet myself
with open arms—
soothe my pain,
wipe my tears.
I must stand tall
and face my battles,
head-on.

I must blow my dream out
and fill the void
with my own essence—
my joy,
my excitement for life.
Every bit of happiness
I grow and nurture
on my own.

Triggers

Fingers stretching for pens.
Fingers tapping on keys.
Never at a loss for words—
reeling as I fall toward earth.

Screaming at the top of my lungs,
"This is enough."
"This IS enough."

With lips sealed shut,
I hear the shrieking all the same—
felt from fingertips
to unrooted toes.

Racing heart,
quick air through nose.
As eyes see stars,
and pinpricks grace arms—

I flip the switch.
The lights are back on.
Hanging in the air once more.

All is calm.

Until I fall.

Clean

Let the feeling wash over me—
and let it go.
It is not mine,
but an illness
that has sunk its claws
into my chest.

Acknowledge it.
Push it away.
It is not me—

I decide
how it touches me.
And it shall not.
No more.

I am mine.

Salt
I feel lighter,
as if a boulder has been
lifted off my shoulders.
I know the opinions of others
shouldn't make me feel so
inescapably smothered.

It's quiet in my brain.
I can hear the soft beckoning of spring—
blue jays chirping from the garden trellis,
the smell of wet dirt,
of soil thawing
beneath the last breath of winter.

My head is mine once more.
I hope to hold onto this feeling,
forevermore.
No more jumbled voices
abounding in my head:
"You aren't good enough."
"You'd be better off dead."

It was a long December.

The whispered promise of spring
guides the last gray tear
down my cheek.
It pools at my feet—
and the rain comes to carry it away,
soaking back into the earth,
once more.

Basking

I may not have
all the answers,
but the person I am today—

is warm,
and full of love.
The person I am today
is the most me
I've ever been.

I fill my time
with people
and hobbies
that bring me joy.

I have boundaries.
And though I may panic
when enforcing them,
I do it anyway.

I love and protect myself
in ways
I was never strong enough
to do before.

I guard my heart.
I meet my needs.
I validate my emotions.

I am me.
I recharge.
I rest.
I laugh.
I play.

I found the light.

Coffee Thoughts

I want home to be tall trees —
strong enough to root me,
to keep me sheltered and safe
from the scorching heat
of summer's hottest days.

I want home to be quiet and sweet —
fingers entangled beneath sheets,
while drifting
off to
sleep.

I want home to be the pitter-patter
of paws and tiny feet —
following me like ducklings,
guided by their mother
toward water.

If all that's missing is the trees,
it still won't quite feel right to me.
One day I awoke,
surrounded by roads —
with no trees to call home.

Home is where my soul glows,
and I can't find it in the pavement —
not without my square of dirt
to dig in,
to root.

Effervescent

Welcome to my eternal iteration
of the same feeling.
The same moments when
my breath would hitch,
the world stopped spinning,
and my heart ceased to beat.

I've written it into oblivion.
I've screamed it—
a beacon into the ether.
It's carved into the bark of billowy trees.
I've spelled it out in the stars,
reflected by moonlight,
on skin, all over me.

Through the haze, it can be read—
a message I once tried to unsend.
And now a new line lingers
in the atmosphere:

I no longer care.

I am a universe in and of myself,
filled to the brim,
with stars dancing in my eyes.
I am the magic,
a phoenix born from the ashes.
I am whole.
I am not hollow anymore.

An Ode to Me

I will not falter.
I will not fall.
I will love myself—
most of all.

Power

You won't find me here.
I disappeared—into the atmosphere.
Free from you at last,
glance at me through glass.

"I am good."
"I am kind."
"I am divine."

Reborn from flame,
I rose from ash.
With an iron grip around my torch,
I declare: this flame is mine.

Follies and Crowns

It was love enduring,
surviving shipwrecks
which should have
left us drowned.

A miracle of second life
led us to hallowed ground.
Hand in hand we stand,
poppy petals falling
like a crown upon my brow.
Yet I hesitate
to sail back into the blue.

Phorcys' Sirens steered our ship
into shallow rocky cliffs.
But Persephone led me
to her poppy garden,
and it's here where I wait.

For what—I can't be certain.
A sign carved on an oar:
"Get back into these waters,
or lament here on the shore."

For cursed are the waters,
haunted by my pain.
I was made of sky and air—
you were born from rain.

I am safe on land,
amongst the flora and the bees.
You would drag me to your boat
on bloody, bent knees.

For it's my love you worship.
It's my crown you fear.
If you drag me to the water,
it's there where you can steer.

I will braid you a crown of gold
if you serenely stay by my side.
But if it's waves you still seek,
I'll watch you from the beach—
the horizon yours to greet.

Space

I will fill my time
with all that is mine.
I sit in the rays of light.
I paint.
I read.
I write.

I.
It's all mine.
It's all me.
Weightless.
Unburdened.
Free.

Watch me finish my climb.
Watch me soar from the peak—
as light as a bird.

My heart is whole.
My heart is mine,
once more.

Enigma

I am a universe,
in and of myself.

Leaving luminescent
fingerprints
on everything I touch.

Irrepressible,
enigmatic,
effervescent,
and incredibly—rare.

Begin Again and Again

Hello, old friends—
trowel and shovel,
seeds and pail.
I think I'm ready to grow again.

I promise to try.
I won't let you die this time.
I'll nurture you—
my sunflowers, zinnias, and delphiniums of blue.

I'll root you where the sun
can always rest upon you.
I'll water you
when the soil runs dry.

I'll watch
the bees and butterflies
find you.

Together,
we begin again.

Welcome Back

Sun warming skin,
soles treading pavement.
Daffodils rise to greet me,
bumblebees hover in the air —

and I made it to this moment.

What a liberating feeling.
My heart is calm.
My thoughts, a bright star —
a beacon of bright days
waiting to be embraced.

Follies and Crowns

Creation

A Canvas

I wish I could paint.
Quaint villages,
filled with tiny cottages,
where hydrangeas—
blue and pink in flowery bunches—
present a perfect welcome
along each side of every front door,
where robin's egg blue shutters
frame each tiny little window.

The village would be fashioned
in a valley of countryside hills,
glistening in the glow of the afternoon sun,
while the bluest of blue skies float above.
The townspeople would walk
along the cobblestones,
carrying perfectly fashioned bouquets in one hand
and wine glasses filled to the brim in the other,
with red wine sloshing
from side to side with their blissful little steps,
their rosy cheeks full of laughter and jest.

What's that up on the hill?
A little family sprawled out on a white blanket,
gathered around a straw picnic basket.
The mother reaches up to hold onto her hat
as a gust of wind blows through,
wrapping her blonde hair around her cheeks
with a smile on her lips.
As the brushstroke of wind sweeps through...

it picks up the corners of the blanket
like it's attempting to take flight.
The little ones are
picking at a bunch of luscious purple grapes,
while the father pours a glass of wine
to share with his wife.

And peeking into the right window
of the cottage at the end of the road,
an elderly woman knits by the window,
a lazy gray cat snoozing on top of her feet,
doing what cats do best—
keeping warm with the woman's body heat.
But little does she know that right next door,
two women are caught in a lovers' tryst,
barely visible through the corner of the left window,
their naked bodies embrace,
planting kisses on each other's face.

A perfect world, tenfold.
This is where I'd go.
I'd brush each stroke
with an impressionist flair.
If I could paint with words,
I'd do it without a care!
A pretty little scene
in the countryside of France,
breathing life into the beauty
of a quaint little village,
filled with tiny cottages

and happy little people.

A muse I can't refuse—
to paint with the most beautiful of hues:
pinks, purples, and blues.
To breathe life into something
and hang it on a wall—
what a talent to have.
I'd paint it all!
To take a picture inside your mind
and bring it into this world—
oh, what a skill I adore.

I'd take us to the depths of the ocean
and then leap up for air.
We'd propel to the sun
and paint the view from there.
Falling back down, we'd capture the stars
like shards of glass,
breaking and bending back and forth,
spilling down upon the ground.
I'd paint each and every single blade of grass.

Looking inward at my soul,
I'd outline the edges
with the warmest of hues.
In the broken pockets,
I'd paint with colors dark as night—
to capture the loss and bitterness
that come with life.
I'd fill in the crevices with the whitest light

to illuminate the hope and optimism
that keep us turning the pages.

To fill in the rest,
I'd start with my breast—
they'd be the lightest of blues, to commemorate
those who have laid upon them and wept.
My shoulders would be the color of stone.
And to end, I'd paint the colors in my head—
an array of pastels flowing to and fro like a river
through a canyon
that has no end.

If I could paint...
I would paint.

Growing

If little me could see this painting,
She'd ask, "You didn't take a class?"
"Are those egg yolks or flowers?"
"Leaves or jalapeños?"
"Is that one a pickle?"
I'd think of all the times
She tried to escape her own mind.
Unfinished stories lost in journals,
Oil paints and easel sold at a garage sale,
Fingers on keyboard keys,
Air pushed through oboe reeds—
All thrown to the wayside
When perfection wasn't easy to achieve.
I'd tell her, "It doesn't matter.
You just pick up the pen or brush,
And let yourself out to breathe.
You don't have to be good at anything."
I'd tell her 5,782 other things too,
But with the concept of time,
I'd say, "You're never alone.
Somewhere down the road,
I wrap my arms around you
And never let you go."

"And when the lights went out,
And I turned blue,
That's when I crawled back to you.
I slayed your monsters,
I took your hand,
And at long last,
I tucked us back into bed—
Again, and again, and again, and again."

Creators

I know it to be true.
In my shadow, I lit a flame.
Beckoning my little moths to me, I sang—
With joviality echoing
Through empty, darkened rooms,
I returned to a vibrant hue.

For isn't joy a sweeter song to sing than sorrow?

Handfuls

She likes to sit and write,
whispering dreams by candlelight,
unmoored, floating toward the moon,
bringing handfuls of stardust back to you—
with no promise of a heart more true
to ever glow so purely for you.

Fragmented Moments

Poems unfold.
Emily Dickinson carries me
to a room of gold.

Birds chirp gaily
through windowpanes,
as dogs sleep at my feet.

Spring waits below.
Bees hum. Roses bud.
The warming air fills my lungs.

Safe

Deepest desires
guide me to
still waters.

Legs crossed,
grass brushing
against my knees.

Sun warming cheeks,
birds chirping melodies
overhead.

Not a moment of reprieve—
but eternity.
A peace all-encompassing.

With a pen in hand,
a notebook resting
on my lap,

Words that are my own
sprawl freely
from my hand.

Scorpio Moon

I do not suffer
for the art of it.
I do not drift in darkness
for the lore of it.
If my soul sinks into the abyss,
I might as well write—
floating in my shadow.

Tumbling

Poetry isn't for everyone,
but it seems to be for me.
No rules.
No constrictions.
My words can flow freely
and carry my convictions.
I don't have an artist's heart—
just scattered thoughts.
It starts to feel like a farce.

My head is full of rainbows
and fields of flowers to paint,
but the talent in my hand
falls flat on the canvas.
Stories run freely through my mind,
but the thought of typing flawless sentences
has me falling over dead.
So, I find myself here—
in a poem once more,
a ruleless terrain.

What more could I ask for?

Follies and Crowns

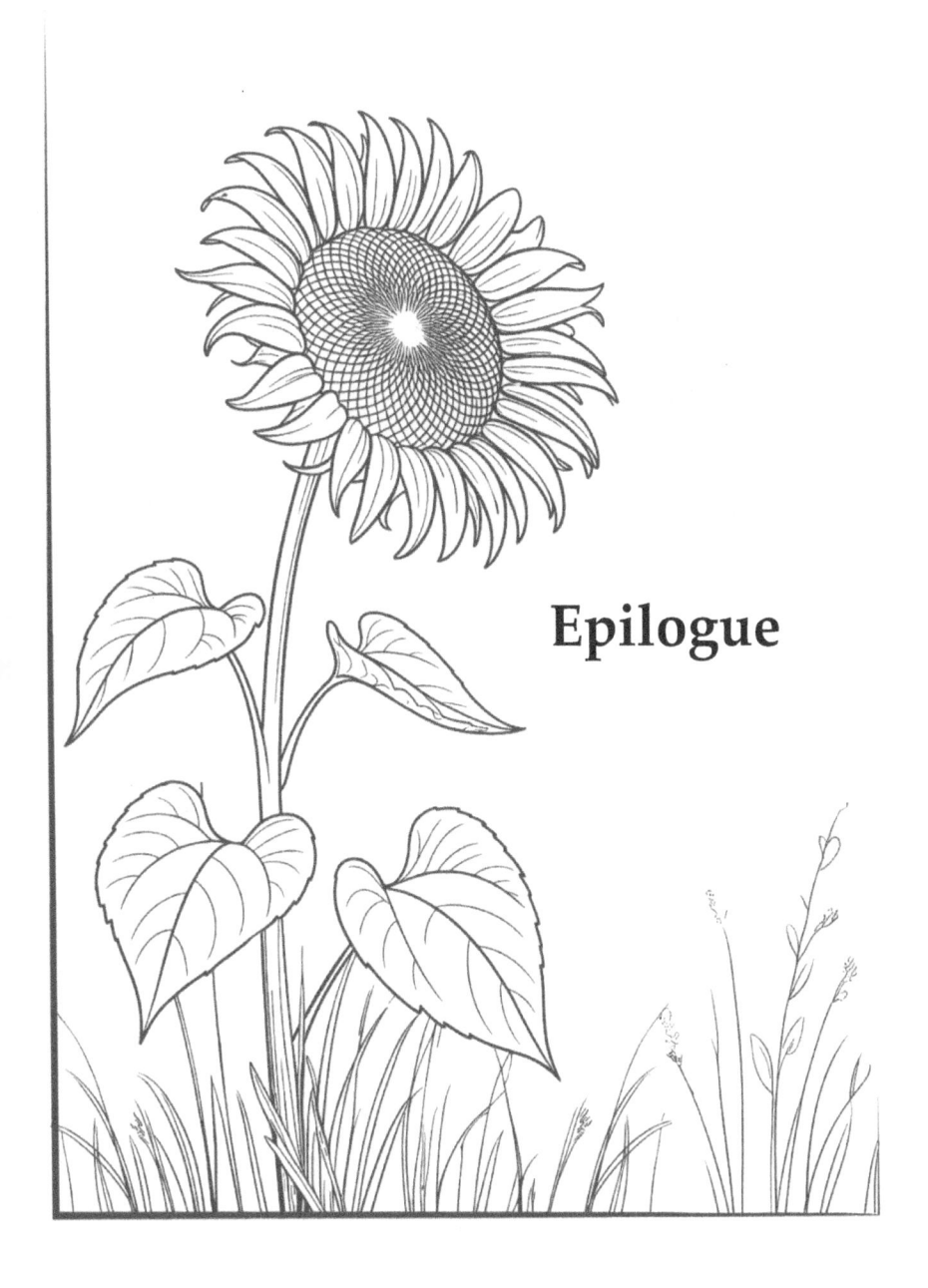

Epilogue

Sunflower

I stretch toward the sun.
I wilt, and I wane.
I absorb the rain.
Standing tall,
I blossom—
golden rays outstretched.

Enduring as summer days pass,
I far surpass the grass.
I offer shelter to bees, shrouded in pollen.
I feed the birds with my seeds.
And when they fall,
nestled into the dirt—

I am reborn.

Acknowledgements

I thank my favorite Cancer for sheltering me during the storm and for giving me the space and peace to find my way back to myself. I thank my favorite Libra for laughing with me and for sharing the silence while simply existing in each other's company. I thank my dogs for rooting me here and for giving me purpose when I wanted to float away. I am eternally grateful for the lights in my life who shone for me as I searched for the match to relight my own.

About the Author

Kayley studied literature in college and through those studies she found poetry to be her favorite form of expression. She lives with her partner, 3 dogs, tuxedo cat, beta fish, and snail. She spends her time frolicking, gaming, gardening, making silly LEGO videos, painting, reading, and writing poetry.

Made in United States
Cleveland, OH
01 August 2025

19043540R00069